INVISIBLE
PARADISE
A COLLECTION OF POEMS
INSPIRED BY FILM

MARC SAVETT

ISBN: 978-0-9988811-6-4

Invisible Paradise/Savett-1st ed.
1. Poems. 2. Poetry. 3. Verse.
4. Savett 5. Film

No Frills Buffalo/Amelia Press
<<<>>>
119 Dorchester Road
Buffalo, New York 14213
For more information please visit
nfbpublishing.com

To my brothers Bill and Noah

Invisible
Paradise

The Poems

LA STRADA FELLINI 1954 OPENING THE MYTHOLOGICAL WORLD

Quinn the strong man loves the story of the circus
Buys a lover from her mother in Fellini's
La Strada glowing fires of the sun pricking
Senses the song of ocean kisses unmeasured
Birth in the abyss solitary assassin of life and

Art blossoms perfumes fragrance that floats
Up through azure wraiths flying above the netting
Below as the acrobats catch and throw themselves
Like lightning through electrical eyes that beacon
Safety for lost sailors portrait of moon sadness
Manakins that move the action along that
Remain motionless hungry for affection
Man eating mares shinny and bay

DARE DEVIL TEST PILOT DIRECTED WILLIAM WYLER 1938

Your thinking was nightly oblique cracking
Ice cubes as B -17's were blowing up over
Iowa flat lands kisses of hard perfume
Pulling down the landing gears I will come to
You in the moon's craters of madness
Azure bouquets are thrown to the abyss
He dies in an emergency landing smelling

Of Alcohol and peril the compliant lover
Of Dare Devils and Werewolves
Crows wings crackle exploding in flame
Too hot for waiting pools dry bones
Waste to dusty oblivion as test pilots
Sip booze crashing into cornfields in Iowa
Myrna Loy blows kisses birthing in that
Abyss sipping absinth asking for the hand
Of the stunt pilot

OK CORRAL TOMBSTONE MY DARLING CLEMENTIME
JOHN FORD 1946

Gunfire blasts from the silver barrel
In that grave yard riding into the death trap
Tombstone a rampage of execution
Wraiths floating over graves
Protector of the badge sorrows sole nobility
Exploring the river of desire wearing a mystics cloth
Killers walking down dreamscapes riflemen
Blast through smoke and mist

The dead knowest no shame or remorse
The cemetery holds the walking dead spirits of the night
Blood soaked ground eremites test in solitude
Uproar of the fast draw perpetuate the fury of our
Fate tooth and nail sharp as steely gunfire
Tears and rends the blossom of the gunfighters creed
Untested gangs of killers walking the gallery
Of death blinded by retorts lost
In smoke coughing for breathe and last
Sustenance

BEAUTY OF LIQUORED NECTAR

Pictorals of hell misery and life's eternal designs
Give suffering as a divine antidote growing intoxicated
Singing the Way of the Cross mobeled in gloom
Unable to arise from the walnut seats struck with black
Stark tumults sucked into the rhythms of Louis Armstrong
Blowing a staccato brass horn into the heavens mirrored night

Face of death brings on the dance them dry mouldering
Bones tip toeing through oblivion rejuvenating dark
Companions Beatles sing their metered cadence
Bound to layers of beauty ambrosia and liquored nectar
The titanic waves swell and break smashing the beachhead
A child is born an elder dies the cycles of life
A spinning Ferris wheel four aces a strait flush
A leopard watches fires splendors

BOGIE TO HAVE AND HAVE NOT HOWARD HAWKS 1944

Private investigator twists turns
Slick racy who done it black mail
Murder decadence lurid beauty
Fox caught in the trap mist shrouded
Hollow eyes wanton lures blood
Flowing from palsied warriors

Obscuring earthly delights
Stepping through clouds of cotton candy
Hot blooded femme fatales high on perfume
And red lipstick immersed in long kisses
Misled deception lies that fall on the floor of broken dreams
Waves breaking on the sand foghorns crying in the dark night

Languorous beauties shadowing
Terrors of ghastly nights that dicks
Prowl with deaths killers' device
Untangling knots of deceit
Angel of beauty knowest wrinkles
With creeping age sphinx undeciphered
Heavens terror of the libertine

BRANDO ON THE WATERFRONT ELIA KAZAN 1954

Song of the sea container ships
Girl friends smile kisses unmeasured
Union hall on the wharf errand boy gets work today
For the mob until he fought the rackets with
His fists lying unconscious on the waterfront
Till the boy man rose up over it like a phantom
Curdled with blood now the rackets exposed
As beauty of the wharf hangs in abeyance

Brando says" I could have had class, I could have been
A contender, I could have been somebody instead of
Of the bum which is what I am" Creed of violence
Sweet wine racketeers floating into grey sky
Gliding wings bills dining on small fish
In the sweep of scythe and sickle
Madrigal of hope and second chances
Duels to the death lost Thrones
Billows swelled to a thousand fires
Extinguished with the divine antidote
Into grey skies seagulls fly free diving into the surf
Lost in the unfurled gathering awaiting the new day

ONCE UPON A TIME IN THE WEST SERGIO LEONE 1968

Tracking the sadistic outlaw who killed his brother
Full cuff of young hips air ominous
Staring at lost dames who step into tiled lobbies
Watching from a fifth floor window playing with the gun in her hand
Hips chiseled shoulders supple running down stairwells

Vengeful curses fatal gibbet hangs as thugs sing death chants
Lovers shield faces fortunetellers climbing ropes to the clouds
Blood gushes in torments like a fountain sobbing
Retorts of gunfire drive the meek home
Feral beasts are on their quarry as the sheriff
Holds his revolver the deadline ticks while a
Flash of pistols crash and bark ominous death

THE KILLERS ROBERT SIODMAK 1946

Without fanfare mob boys burst into the juke joint
Looking for revenge a nasty mug Swede involved in a heist
With a jig saw of intrigue and bloody mouth of revenge
Tentacles contagion revamped in vice and numbers
The bawdy house beckons a sheltered secret coffin
Vengeful love unsated a deck of flashbacks shady gangsters
Glued to the backdrop of the noir air ominous impending danger

The boxer punch drunk in his corner
Bouncing into the twelfth round
Blood gushes its colors looking for redemption
Death's revenge unsolved in tangled puzzles
Looking into the blood shot killers eyes
Cornerman working cuts payroll heist unsolved
Tangled puzzle botched robbery running to ruin
Beauty of courtesans' flowers of evil hide dolorous secrets
Assassins parlay for answers with dark companions

THE MAN WHO FELL TO EARTH Nicholas Roeg 1976
Adaption of the Walter Tevis novel with David Bowie

An alien inconspicuously falls through the atmosphere
To Earth finding he can communicate through
Speech and sign language believing earthlings
Have good senses of humor enjoying company
Laughing heartily with other earthlings who
Seem to be sensitive to emotions and
They are particularly adept at problem solving
The alien Stephen traveled the solar system
For 5 centuries before he landed on earth the
Third planet in the solar system where he
Found a viable water source for his civilization
Stephen introduced new technologies to earth
Though many aliens became dependent on alcohol
And other substances of abuse partying brought many
Aliens and earthlings together cooperating to better
Understand their advanced technologies, water supplies
Were adequate though the climate was slowly changing
From humid to desert conditions
Soft chambers of exhaled oxygen perked up bouquets of Lilies
Soft pleasure is the fragrance of the rose

SHANGHAI EXPRESS JOSEF VON STERNBERG 1932

That face of darkness and light
Her complexion enigmatic shimmering in gradations
Dietrich's face shadows reverberating shadows
Lost in vapors hypnotic perfumes form womens
Wanton lures. Benefactors exploring
Rivers of desire languorous angel of beauty
Eyes eternal splendor
Kisses measured
Goddess of love and trains
Engines howl and wail inside roses thick perfume
Billows swelled a thousand fires and smoke
Secret isles of green myrtle
Come to me sweet love

SWINGTIME ROGERS-ASTAIR 1936

Smiles smirk smoking waltz time
Bojangles in Harlem dressed in blackface
Jaw dropping smoothness tapping on clouds
Gravity turned upside down
Mysterious lightness
World of beauty coming to flower
Feet flashing in moonlight
Sounds and perfume reflect heavens mirrored face
Angels of midnight flying across rooftops
Tightropes of harmony transformed to sound and perfume
Crystal essence of dance tapping on clouds

DETOUR B FILM EDGAR GULMET 1945

Simple insignificant turn on a lost highway
Cheap unfinished veneer death's dissolution
Left hand turn to murder
In a sleazy motel telephone
Cord wrapped tightly round her neck
Shrill company of the edgy hitchhiker
Incriminated with bad luck vibes
Driver suddenly dies from an infarction
Hitchhiker looking for West Coast Swing jazz musician
Meets loser after loser driving him mad
Unhinged pessimism
Like a Japanese steak knife through the heart
He knows the enchantress of dark midnight
Gehenna's miseries howl and scream

POSTMAN ALWAYS RINGS TWICE TAY GARNETT 1946

Cora is drawn quick and hard to Frank
Lives in a roadside diner with Cecil
Her former male companion
Film noir thick raw unrelenting
Frank and Cora swim in the moonlight breakers
Doomed affair founded on murder
Cecil wacked by Chambers
Cora killed in crash
Frank is executed
They played their roles lost in confusion and smoke
Tear and rend blossom of lovers call
Scars from loves talons sweet wine orchards
Fragrance hypnotic walking through clouds of lavender
Sorrows sole nobility what could have been
Tear and rend blossoms of lovers calling
Sucked into deep grottos with the crumbling dead

THE BIG SLEEP HOWARD HAWKS 1946

Double crossed boilerplate noir private investigators
Blackmailed beauty and the beast
Mists of west coast racy dialogue
Gunshots wake cops the dead supine in the street
Beauty and the beast my dear
Women coming to flower beauty of form and soft whispers
Terrors of ghastly night lightning through electric eyes

Waves crashing on beach mired in secret affections
Flat foot investigates noir terrors snub nose five shot revolver
Depth of misery coming to flower form sound and perfume
Reflected in the breakers like pistols cracking in the night
Forever secrets gnawing flayed hearts in depths of misery
Coming to flower poets of pleasure
Mirrored face reflected in heavens
Gunfire through the mist chased by worms dark companions
The dead scream into the black night

DOUBLE INDEMNITY TAY GARNETT 1946

Husband tricked into signature for a policy that pays double
If death occurs on a train
MacMurray the claims investigator is head over heels for Phyllis
Encountering each all over town till they have succeeded
Pounding each other with bullets before MacMurray
Stumbles into an insurance company doorway gravely injured
Dictating a confessional on the Dietrichson claim
Dying in his partners arms sniffing the flowers of evil
Upturned eyes steal a glance secret splendor and fatal beauty
Loves infidelities carved in stone spirits lost in the night
Ineluctable chords in harmony

MANCHURIAN CANDIDATE 1962

Brain washed son surrounded by Chinese Communists
Assassination attempts by zombie warriors
Son of US Scion trained in mind control
Political ops kill as they were instructed
Walking with chips in their brains plastic lures hollow
warriors
Pulp SiFi end of Korean conflict
Wiles with haunted eyes
Wolves incubated in lair
Plastic lures hollow warriors phantoms of the night
Desecrated virtue dark companions
Worms shrouded in horrors mist

VIRIDIANA 1961
BUNUEL

Viridiana is visited by her uncle who
Becomes excited by the resemblance.
To his ex- wife and decides to rape her,
And then kills himself.
Viridiana enters a convent and
Becomes co-heir to his estates.
A gorgeous spring rose
She adopts a band of whores beggars and thieves
Benevolence leading to disaster and
Self-destruction in a moving panorama.
A Ferris wheel of earthly delights
She is transformed knowing
Pain suffering and charity
As a divine antidote to sloth
And worms that wait in her sleep

LAS HARDES BUNUEL 1933
LAND WITHOUT BREAD

Harsh conditions usher in malnutrition
And starvation's streets
Urchins with four teeth in their mouth
Youngsters on the brink of existence
Stark juxtaposition between riches of church
And poverty living in squalor
Stuff of suffering, nightmares, starvation
Skewed De Profundis
Ghoulish labors living on cliffs of oblivion
Halls of misery puzzles of nightmares
Death and despair running
Before the cougars scream
Sleeping on piles of bones
Speaking with heavenly angels

AFRICAN QUEEN
JOHN HUSTON 1951

Adventure love story between Bogart
And Hepburn German warship blocks
Escape route. They ride on good vibes
World of beauty orchids jungle perfumes
Dark love breaths nectar eyes steal glances
Upturned lips smiles sweet and tender
Suffered terrible pleasures splendid
Taste of jungle nectar guilty trysts
Eyes contact splendid beauty
Satisfaction joys broad smiles
Walking tight ropes with birds of paradise
Langorous solitude gorgeously
Moulded dark love WW1 sweet delight
Bogart and Hepburn breathe jungle fragrances
Arms outspread dark love secret attraction

UNBERTO D
VITTORIO DE SICA 1952

In both cases love and attachment
Were the most important factors
Within each individuals life. The retired professor
Ballisti and Flike his dog were sole companions.

There is a strong devotion between man and animal
They both kept the other alive with
Within their invisible essential kinship
They both lived together in meager circumstances
Angels of Kindness float above them
Both are satisfied in an invisible paradise
Each devoted to the other in love and kindness
Giving both strength to prepare for tomorrows challenges

LOS OLVIDADOS THE YOUNG AND THE DAMNED
LUIS BUNUEL 1950

Slums of Mexico City smells of decay and decadence
Dreams of poetic irrationality as the Angel
Of Death walks down dark roads
The street gangs caustic and unrelenting
Gangsters run reform schools ghoulish labors
Grotesque unrequited essence of degeneration
Imprisoned in a moving panorama of filth and sloth
Oblivion Queen of Pollution blows fires across the sun
Evidence of the gangsters crumbling existence
They vie for position murdering monsters in the night
Down country roads with automobile accidents
As crumpled borders winds kiss heavens
Mirrored face from all sides
Naked slaves languish in grottoes oblivion

CASABLANCA
MICHEAL CURTIZ 1942

Turbulent Epic Sam plays as time goes by on piano
"Claude rains says round up the usual suspects "Rains
Again Louis I think this is the beginning of a
Beautiful friendship" Nazi reunions infect from the inside
Like a plague
Teardrops fall not a dry eye as the plane lifts off the ground
Enchantress of dark midnights wooed into forgetfulness
Nazi collaborators percolate through the hotel
World of dreams and beauty
Air ominous with thick soft secrets
Antidotes to life's suffering
Ambrosias nectar carries dark forebodings
Through the clouds

HAXAN
BENJAMIN CHRISTENSON 1923
SILENT FILM

Explores witchcraft misunderstandings
Regarding mental illness blends facts with mythologies
Preoccupations with demons witches and devil possession
"We no longer burn our old and poor, though they
Do suffer bitterly" Parade of demons and spirits
Gehenna place of misery. "Wraiths
Breaking hearts narrated by William Burroughs"
Convulsive tumults hum oblivions song
Enchantress born of dark midnights
Study of misery and mental deformations
Lost in oblivion crumbling in decay and putrescence

AN ANDULUSIAN DOG
LUIS BUNUEL 1928

EARLY SURREALISM

Collaboration with SALVADOR DALI

Dali slices open a dogs eye, is this action
More egregious than the spectacle of a cloud veiling
The moons' deep forces of the ID While
Forces of EGO impart inspiration and discovery.
Passion cannot sate the vengeful lover

The heart of the bird flutters
Inside the body of secret fires
In the deep spring where mysteries abound
Incongruous disconnected images
Fragments of the unconscious
Churning forces within
ID and EGO vie for sustenance
Lightning flashes against the black sky

L'AGE D'OR LOUIS BUNUEL 1930

Opens with documentary on scorpions
Starving bandits, four bishops fade to skeletons
Sequences set for elegant party at the villa.
Violence between surrealists interfere with the reception
Images of a cow on the bed viewed as
Desecration of earthly beauty
The dying phantom searches for splendor
In the night of jewels and silver
Flashes of lightening across
Grey skies cracking with thunder

ALL QUIET IN THE WESTERN FRONT
LEWIS MILESTONE 1930

Depiction of tragedy WW1
Gas masks death in trenches
Schoolboys disillusioned
By horror death and destruction
World of beauty convulsing
Ghoulish labors come to flower
Mists shrouded by bomb blasts flesh
Blown up into atmosphere gas sucking breath
Languishing in foxholes choked by tendrils miseries
Despair like worms putrescent
Vanished and deceased dark companions
Dying phantoms war is suffering in gloom
Nails hammer sharp points into the heart

I AM A FUGITIVE FROM A CHAIN GANG
MERVYN LEROY 1932 PAUL MUNY

Searing indictment of penal practices
World War1 Vet railroaded into shackles
And hard labor in Deep South
Splitting rocks pursued by bloodhounds

Away into the nights terrible darkness
Twisted running to ruin
Living in ominous solitude harsh labors
Breaking up rock one day after the next
Sisyphus with never ending labors
A bear protesting the trap
A ghost wasting to night

SUNSET BLVD BILLY WILDER 1950

Unemployed screen writer floating in swimming pool
Recounts doomed involvement with Norma Desmond
Living in decaying mansion on Sunset Boulevard
Norma Desmond kills Joe Gillis with a handgun
Norma is played by Gloria Swanson
Dreams of a comeback pedicured manicured mega facials
"I am big the pictures got small "
During her arrest she walks
Toward the camera holding her pose
Emphasing her isolation and mental illness as Joe
Floats face down on the swimming pool
He recalls playing and dancing with a pet chimpanzee
Divine virtues forever bound to his swimming pool tomb
Joe lost in oozing algae slime never believing Norma's
Potential for psychosis an enchantress bursting to flame

A PLACE IN THE SUN
AMERICAN TRAGEDY 1951 ADAPTED FROM
THEODORE DRIESER'S 1925 NOVEL

Courtroom drama played out in Central New York
Stuck in thankless job dominated by insecurity
Impregnates girlfriend, Grace tense alone
Depends on Chester to stay, Grace threatens to leave him
Grace drowns under suspicious circumstances
Chester makes a feeble attempt at
Best to save her smitten by the
Taylor Character. Chester Gilette is tried for Murder

Convicted of drowning Grace Brown
Whose overturned canoe
Was found in Big Moose Lake.
Love letters to Gillette were read in court
Chester Gilette died in an electric chair in Auburn prison
He was ringing Salvation Army bells on
The streets prior to moving to New York
Never quite gaining his place in the sun the overturned boat,
Dreams of beauty smashing life's eternal designs
Worms crawling through tunnels dark companions singing
The way of the cross spirits vain snatching at the sky
The impregnated woman, his poor work history.
His ghoulish labors

THE HUSTLER ROBERT ROSSON 1961

Newman plays Fat Eddie Felson cocky pool shark
Bitter cynical portrayal excluding all things from your life
Pool is the universe. Smoky back- drop distant relationship
Ambivalent alcoholic love interest
George Scott tries to keep it cool at the table
Loyalty lasting as long as the balls fall in the corner
Pocket and the booze stays in the cupboard
Broken hands dark companions
Phantom of the left corner pocket
Crystals to ruin black stark tumults snatching at the sky
His hands hobbled and crumbling with lost focus at the table
The cold grandeur of sinking
Thirty balls in a row then running
All the balls on the table before a sip of hard whisky

THE BURMESE HARP KON ICHIKAWA 1956

Displayed equal artistry an elegy for lost
Innocence Captain Inouye
Leads a platoon into Burma a mix of
discipline and musical instruction
Inouye's harp player agrees to speak with conscripts rather
Than allowing death on the artillery range
Mizushima awakens, assumed lost, realizes a higher purpose
Garbed as a Buddhist Monk the injured
Set about burying the dead
Across south East Asia an act of God living a renewed life
A lasting tribute to the dead both
Innocent guilty good and evil
The wings of the bird flutter, the sky opens, the golden light
Warms the future our dead are buried
Tribute to the dead and turbulent labors
Which becomes a beam of light shot to the heavens
Ambrosia plays with clouds and wind

TREASURE OF THE SIERRA MADRE B TRAVEN AUTHOR
JOHN HUSTON 1948
B TRAVEN Wrote DEATH SHIP

American drifters prospect for gold
B Traven novel filmed in Mexico
Dry air grit stuck between the teeth
Pounding rock all day for gold dust
Bogart paranoid that his buddies are stealing his gold
Which begins to blow away
From his saddlebags in an afternoon gale
Bandits close in like a hive of wasps on Bogart
Pounding gold rock all day for
Months losing focus on the prize

Bandits devouring every last bit of the prospectors dust
Teeth and nails sharp as steel rending the blossom
Of youth running to ruin twisted by the lure of gold
Greed's claw destroyed the cohesiveness of the
Prospectors stake some losing all based on insanity
Running to ruin twisted in lure of gold
Rending the blossom of youth
Slaves languishing in deep grottos
Flowers of misery paranoia and oblivion
We live in our disguise losing humanity
Can we cope with bats flying down our throats?

Nuit et Brouiilard FOG AND NIGHT 1955

Documentation on Holocaust horrific events
Time dilutes memory a reminder of
What mankind is capable of
Black and white archival footage of camps
Absolute brutality mass graves corpses hung on
Barbwire fences concentration and labor camps

Skeletal nude bodies gas chambers and crematoriums
Nazi's deny culpability black and
White footage inside camp
In reutilization of discarded
Items i.e. hair, shoes, gold and teeth
The most brilliant minds lost to worms and oblivion
Dying with insects and rodents a desecration of
Humanity evidence of insanity that men could do this to
Other men suffering in life's brutalities

GUYS AND DOLLS
JOSEPH L MANKIEWIZ 1955

Engaging musical with blockbuster characters
Gambler Sky Masterson [Brando] talked {Simmons]
Into flying to Havana for a nightcap Damon Runyan's
Tales of lobable streetwise crooks with NYC speech

Slang and behavior Sky caught in dance passions
Simmons lost in rum and coke secrets wearing soft masks
Holding lovers in their arms evening doves
Cooing soft whispers in their ears
Form rosebuds cadenced meters beauty and song
Dancing in ambrosia and perfume

GRAPES OF WRATH-JOHN STEINBECK
JOHN FORD 1940

Coping with walls of dust choking
Thick clouds suffocating clogging
The airways blocking vision growing
Season withered and wilted
Land desolate and barren families banded together traveling
To California to find work picking fruit living in squatter camps
Though the government pays starvation wages
Families such as the Joads
Spoke out for better working conditions
Claiming" were the people we'll go on
Forever "Madrigal of sorrow
Moonflower indistinguishable humanity lost in solitude harsh
Labors losing all possessions dear, dark companions piercing
Torments vain writhings crumbling memories

THE BAKERS WIFE---MARCEL PAGNOL 1938

Based on short story by Jean Givno
Tale of a baker in a small provincial village
Young wife deserts husband for a
Handsome shepherd. When the baker ceases
Baking, village functions are halted.
Villagers forget feuds and focus on
Bringing home the wife. Pognot animates a galaxy of
characters. Each character
Has a defined role an elemental magnetism slowly brought
Back together to weave a grand pattern
Drawn back together coming to flower
With interwoven beauty

THE GOOD THE BAD THE UGLY SERGIO LEONE 1966

Clint Eastwood was invited to Italy to
Remake Akira Kurosawa's
Movie Yojimbo The Good Bad and the Ugly
Including radical editing
Techniques. The graveyard scene suggests
A Greek stage drama
With marble sandstone and granite. Ennio Morricone's
Music provides intriguing instrumentation
Including electric guitar
And whistles the focus on the stage are the
Three faces Eastwood, Van Cleef and Wallach
This panorama of eyes, and facial expressions
Accentuates the fast draw
The good bad and ugly battle in a moving
Panorama coming to flower
A wolf caught in a trap hardboiled gunslingers western drawls
And steely1957 navy revolvers fire of
The sun pricking the black abyss

SEREI M EISENSTEIN 1927

Eisenstein presented his film Battleship Potemkin.
Massive crowd scenes were organized. Although the film
Was hard to follow, October was his masterwork
Ambitious and powerful. He understood that editing was an
Artform independent and fundamental
Sections of film joined together a new world coming
To flower fusing sections of film in myriad combinations
Eisenstein was the cinema's most remarkable personality
For the first fifty years of cinema.
The mystical interaction occurs
When two separate pieces of film are joined together
He imagined that cinema could represent visual thinking
Scratch below the films surface and feel a touch of madness

JFK 1961 JOHN F KENNEDY ASSASINATION 11/22/63

Many possible directions weaving
A case for conspiracy theories
Many possibilities, but in the end
Warren Commission, Jim Garrisons
Theorizing, home movies by Zapruder, though there was a
Mountain of evidence. The country experienced misery
Suffering, gloom, laughter died with no antidote for a
Population mobeled in sadness this an evil deed with no
Answers or resolution. The country experienced
Misery and suffering laughter died

DRIVE NICOLAS WINDING REFN 2011

Adapted from 2005 novel by James Sallis
Getaway expert hypnotic picture of death and destruction
Fairy tale noir pure pulp, taking the foot off the accelerator
Slamming the foot down an the
Pedal listening to Stealers Wheel
Looking at a knot of vipers sons of
Putrescence and a thousand fires
Speeding though city scapes putting the pedal to the metal
Stunt driver slamming on the
Accelerator Bryan Cranston mentor
And father figure mixture of
Love death sensuality romance tension
Head-crunching action influences
Include Alejandro Jodorowsky
Characters transformed by violence
Both grotesque and beautiful
Gosling plays mechanic, stunt driver and getaway expert

TOUCH OF EVIL ORSON WELLES 1958

Noir of strip joints motel rooms of sleaze depravation
And corruption a bomb planted in a convertible
Explodes while the Angel of Death knows favors in the night
Warriors run together jousting in smoke filled rooms
Shuffling decks of cards the Joker laughs at them
Death knows fevers in the night
An enchantress rends the way to the heart
Intoxicated in crystal coffins drunken sailors are
High on hard liquor and ambrosia
Meth labs dot the landscape while pranksters
Rule the night as the devils sink their
Teeth into crimes exposed underbelly

INGMAR BERGMAN 1957
THE 7TH SEAL

Black robed white face of death playing chess on a beach
Sydow returns from the crusades
Surprised by con men selling
Corpses explaining God is a disease that must be rooted out
Sydow is fearful
Of the plague by joining the dance of death contemplating the
Stars and sea horrors countless shot from my eyes as the
Deceased night languishes till morning light
Weaving a mystics crown harpies talons grab at the breast
Trembling bursts of flame across dark heavens while
crusades face the grim reaper
She lives while secrets gnaw tomorrow and tomorrow

THE HAUNTING OF HILL HOUSE 1959

Shirley Jackson published the Haunting of Hill House in 1959
Considered to be the scariest film of all time.
Hill house built by a crazed
Individual eighty years earlier with
Four known deaths associated
There began banging noises cold spots
Dr. Markway's wife shows
Up losing control of the car dying after smashing into a tree
Bones sleep in slothful oblivion life
Chants beyond time in grottos
Bats flock seeking caverns in the night with
The enchantress born of dark midnights
Sweeping death from her home holding deaths deformities

THE SNAKE PIT Anatole Litvak 1948

Early psychiatric interventions included power
Hoses insulin shock and electric shock treatment
Olivia de Havilland played a psychiatric patient
In the Snake Pit where individuals underwent
Talking cures, also talking cures appeared in the film
One Flew Over the Cuckoo's Nest,
Many patients were warehoused in psychiatric
Hospitals for extended periods with
Severe psychosis and mental illness
Patients have been treated with break through
Medications resulting in significant
Remission of illness in the last
Thirty years while in patient stays are
Accepted treatment, cognitive behavioral approaches
Behavioral therapies and interpersonal
Therapy have been beneficial
With advent of newer medications there are
More discharges to the community

WHOS AFRAID OF VIRGINIA WOOLF MIKE NICHOLS 1966

Portrait of Taylor and Burton playing
Destructive mental fencing
With younger faculty projecting own personal failures
Expressing self hate before the night is over all parties
Must look inward into their own souls
To excise guilt solitude and
Destructive love hate games projecting personal failures
Mental weakness coping with jibes and jives absorbed at the
Parties biting sarcasms, the fountain
Gushes as a torrent sobbing
Life's blood streams flowing over
Ugly trysts gorged on and picked over
Like extinct Jurassic birds looking for
New thrills and excitements
That turn to terrible pleasures

BATTLE OF ALGIERS GILLO PONTECOVO 1965

Electrifying thriller recounting Algerian struggle
Action takes place between 1954 and 1962
Music by Ennio Marricone film wears
Anticolonialist heart on sleeve
For independence from France
Horrifying killings assassinations
Bombings, Partisans antifascist Resistance
In Italy through WW2 recounting the Algerian struggle
For independence, twisted and skewed horrors
In Italy WW11 Dark companions shot from my eyes
Crumbling streets ordinance exploding
Death before the doorway human cost transformational
Existence slipping through checkpoints
Reprisals and atrocities
Assassins of life and art float up though
An unsettled cloud of uncertainty

THE SHOP ON MAIN STREET KADER AND KLOS 1965

Holocaust drama German occupied Czechoslovakia
Tono the carpenter is pushed to make money by his wife
Collaborating with the Germans in a small Jewish shop run by
A senile woman supported by other Jews
He agrees to be appointed Aryan controller but the shop
Makes no money spending time with a senile woman
Tono agrees to look after this woman a Jew, then an order
Is issued that all Jews will be deported to a labor camp
The woman becomes combative Tono locks her in a closet
The harsh interactions result in the women's death
Circumstances forced Tono to choose and act
My heart frozen in ice and snow tears falling
Death is a miniseries written on a brick wall
Lost in a battle of life's eternal designs
There is a thin line between life and death and
Dreams and madness
Two warriors spangle the air with sparks and splatter

ELTOPO ALEJANDRO JADOROWSKY 1970

Gun fighter sets out to defeat greatest gunslingers to
Achieve enlightenment journeying across a land
Of gangs warriors each symbolizing
Stages of man's enlightenment
Parades of biblical Freudian and Jungian symbols
Bereft and empty of achieving his
Goals with the weight of the world on his back
To protect the deformed
Vulnerable crippled, making a last sacrifice
Protesting war the destruction cycle life death and rebirth
Neath the sky of flaming sun shuddering obscene labors
Phantoms flying through marble skies
Grottos sleep in slothful oblivion
Searching for the void
Neath the sky of flaming sun

INVASION OF THE BODY SNATCHERS
DON SEIGLE 1956 DONALD SUTHERLAND

Science fiction terror cold war allegory
Slimy plant pods that absorb animal existence
Bursting open revealing two replica humans
Town's population assimilated by pods
Devouring flesh Miles the doctor wanders onto the highway
As a pod falls out the back of a tractor trailer
Shouting' your next' horrors countless shot from my eyes
Worms dark companions Gehanna place of hell
Languishing in slime enveloped in flesh devouring pods
Similar to the venus flytrap and the
Pitcher plant both flesh eaters
Threat of invasion inside and outside community

MODERN TIMES—CHARLES CHAPLIN 1936

Chaplin's silent film era portrayed the character of the
Little Tramp in the aftermath of the Great Depression
Confronting themes of poverty, intolerance, and economic
Tyranny of the machine, problems Chaplin
Was acutely aware of during the course of his world
Tour observing social inequalities of unemployment
Depression and automation
Believing machines should benefit the workers
Chaplin exposed problems under the searchlight
Of comedy transforming the little tramp into a
Mere cog working in a factory driven crazy by
Manmade working conditions
Monotony, inhuman workdays, men treated like guinea
Pigs on conveyer belt, flawed approaches leading to
divisiveness
Working inside a pressure cooker
Modern times show Chaplin at his unrivaled peak
Billows swelled a thousand fires splendor

NIGHT AT THE OPERA MARX BROTHERS
SAM WOOD 1935
A PERSONAL INTERPRETATION

Crowds gathering in the ships cabin snaking
Single file for thirty minutes
Repeating itself to perpetuity as if struck down
By Psychic injury to the funny bone unable to move
Caught in the wild passions of the Marx Brothers
Harpo, Chico and Groucho brought one down to one's knees
Groveling in laughter machine gun one liners
Groucho's Distortions Deconstructions and
Corruptions are must see for excruciatingly hilarious comedy

THE LAST PICTURE SHOW
PETER BAGDONOVICH 1971

McMurtry's novel is a coming to age novel set in
A small Texas town with characters trying to find
Their place in a changing world innocence finding
Experience through an assortment of interactions
That leads to finding individual and group strength
The director plays with characters like a chessboard
Quite sure of which direction he is moving in
He attempts to find a seat in changing mores
And interests there is sad reminisce between
The past and present generations of filmmaking
Black and white movies are emotive and striking
Incisive actors and directors will move this generation's
Moviemakers forward with new innovations
And casts of exciting characters the sky billows
To a thousand fires coming to flower pleasures
Mirrored face reflecting the moon

LIFE OF EMILE ZOLA WILLIAM DIETERLE 1937

In prosperous old age Alfred Dryfus
A French army officer was falsely
Accused of spying for the Germans then
Was exiled to Devil's Island victim of
Anti-Semitic prejudice --Warner Brothers feared in 1937
Arising tide of anti-Semitism
Zola was a major figure in liberalization of France
He was nominated for the Nobel Prize in 1901 and 1902
He was a major figure in the exoneration of Alfred Dryfus
Devils Island was a death trap, where he was devoured by
Insects, disease, and living in squalor
While in Europe Dryfus was ironically exposed to a faulty
Heater leaking carbon monoxide killing Dryfus
Heartless labors modeled in gloom worms dark companions

NO COUNTRY FOR OLD MEN
ETHAN AND JOEL COEN 2007

Josh Brolin [Llewelyn Moss] a Vietnam Vet
Stumbles upon a satchel
Containing over two million dollars
Llewelyn Moss takes the satchel, which sets events in motion
Sheriff Bell [Tommy Lee Jones] pursues his quarry working
On unraveling the meaning of these killings
The dead lay around the heroin stash pursued
By hit man Anton Chigurh [Javier Bardem]
Bardem wants the money and goes on a savage shooting
Spree with his shotgun he is gravely injured though
Puts himself back together after visiting a pharmacy
Much of action takes place in a hotel where Bardem
Has constructed sinister devices to kill his pursuers
Who try to bargain with
Woody Harrelson and Kelly Macdonald
This is a tale of killers who beg for time
"You don't have to kill me"
It seems as if the sheriff ages before our eyes
Stunned by the insanity of these killers
Chords of rich harmony life's eternal designs
Horrors countless the vanquished
And deceased dark companions slothful oblivion
Looking into the eyes of the apocalypse
This movie is a beautiful meditation on aging and death

STRANGER ON A TRAIN ALFRED HITCHCOCK 1951 PATRICIA
HIGHSMITH RAYMOND CHANDLER

[Guy Haines, Farly Granger] bump into passenger
[Robert Walker, Bruno Anthony]
Both would like to be without someone in their lives.
Bruno devises perfect murder.
They swap victims. Guy initially Brushes off the idea but
Bruno is black mailing Haines.
Walker's game turns to madness murder and
Blackmail Granger is flamboyant
Guy wants his wife wacked.
Bruno wants his father killed. Haines is a famous tennis
Star late for his match. He starts his game though
There is confusion on the tennis court.
Guy jumps on the carousel and begins punching
Bruno as the Carousel turns faster children
Scream thrown to the ground the police
Intervene to stop the mayhem while
Horses lose their riders because of the terrific
Centrifugal force of the carousel finally
Losing speed when the motor slows
Seething with blasphemies billows swell to a thousand fires
Splendors ineluctable chords.
Secret designs of the queen of pollutions

EL LABERINTO DEL FAUNO PAN'S LABYRINTH GUILLERMO del TORO 2006

Ofelia discovered a world of forest
Creatures that interacted with the child
There were times of harsh interactions
When troops marched through her land
At times her family had great difficulty
Coping with her withdrawn feelings
It was then when she could see
Her forest friends and she spoke by name with her
Creatures of the wood speaking with
The life like creatures that made her feel safe
Losing herself she found herself when
She became confused. Her secret places
Made her feel strong when the army
Pushed fun at her finding strength in her mind
The Angel of beauty knows sorrow and the seas laughter.

THERE WILL BE BLOOD PAUL THOMAS ANDERSON 2007

Excruciating study of greed constructive
And deconstructive powers
Of competiveness and ambition with strong will to dominate
Delves into depths of the antihero
Through madness greed violence
And heartlessness turning resources to
His own boutique through
Madness Paranoia and rock solid decision making
He worked in the oil fields where a rig could blow any time
Could cope with a zealots anger and death
His own temper was thunder and lightening
The spirits vain search for the void
Bones lie in the street chewed by salivating devil dogs

DJANGO UNCHAINED QUENTIN TARANTINO 2012

Elements of Sergio Corbucci's cowboy films
And elements of spaghetti
Western placed in American South Pre Civil War Dr. King
{Christoph Waltz}
A bounty hunter, teaches etiquette
Comfort within the plantation
Django is successful also having bounty
Hunting skills delivering
Corpses paying the bounty hunter cash for
Outstanding bounties
Yearly Greenville slave auction mentioned
As a diversion from
The plantations grisly tortures included castration,
And burning testicles with hot poker as punishment
A blood soaked revenge movie elucidating the concept of
Freedom for bounties.
"If slave was owned by Dicky Mining Co

He breaks rock everyday all day." If a man didn't pay his fees
He could set his dogs on the man." Django tells King of
Broomhilda her German American-roots
King paid 12,000 for Brunhilde's freedom
If plantation etiquette was ignored
A man or woman could be thrown
In the hot box. Flyers in hand would
Show the price of The bounty
For example Smitty Bandy corpses were sold for 7000 dollars.
Place of hell Site of misery suffering living in the void
Of hopelessness inside 5x6 boxes
Vipers imprisoned in ghoulish labors
Life and death depend on the Cotton Baron
Hollow eyes palsied warriors the female's wanton lures
Mist shrouded mansions A man could pay for his freedom
If he paid for his bounty.

INGLOURIOUS BASTARDS QUENTIN TARTINTINO 2009

Inspired by Znzo-Castellar's 1978 The Inglorious Bastards
Brad Pit leads US soldiers through waves of Nazi Soldiers
A young Jewish women's family was murdered before her eyes
She hatches a plot to kill Hitler with her
African lover and Beloved Cinema
Christoph Waltz plays the sadistic Colonel Hans Landa known
As the Jew Hunter for his ability to sniff and snuff out Jews
Landa is cunning and complicated with a genius performance
Climbing under the foundation of the house and rotting timbers
Hearing the footsteps above the floor silent waiting the next move

Anxious she makes a run through the long grasses of the field
A bullet whistles past her left ear as she falls to the ground
Several Nazis are walking along a desolate railroad
She gains confidence from her contacts with the enemy
Revenge lives inside her, evil is all around her
Painting on the houses surrounded by evil flowers
Coping with the dark companions sorrows sole nobility
The theatre is her pride, where she feels most comfortable She
Hatches a plot to kill Hitler with her girlfriend,
African lover, and her beloved
Cinema. She becomes an invisible force that destroys the Nazi's.
Tensions evoke strong emotions, relaxed and at ease,
Her confidence sustains her midst the
Unpredictable interactions with The Nazi officers

CIDADE DE DEUS FERNANDO MEIRELLOS AND KATIA LAND
2002

A Brazilian housing project was
Tracked from the idyllic beginnings
In the 60's to the 80's. Poverty soaked
Into the ground. With poverty
Came violence, crime and instability.
The family unit weakened and
Gun injuries became common.
Outcomes resulting in hospitalization
Took men out of the workforce.
Children of the streets were
Common a decade ago,
Now street violence is less common.
Buscape once photographed in the streets
Is now a successful photographer.
Now adolescents are looking for
Work and placement climbing the corporate ladder
Lilies blow their perfume through the clouds

WAGES OF FEAR HENRI GEORGES CLOUZET 1963

Two teams compete to transport a load of nitroglycerin
Along a 300 mile mountain pass to quench an oil refinery
Fire so they can blow the pipeline. The nitro is excruciatingly
Sensitive to sudden movements and dislocations of the cargo
Clouzet throws as many obstacles in the way of the trucks
As possible over the bumpy mountain highway. The two
Drivers risk their lives for cash. If one truck blows
The other may explode resulting in a no win situation.
The drivers are exploited by their impoverished situation

BAD LANDS TERRANCE MALICK 1979

Kit and Holly have antisocial streaks
Looking for a gun fighter's reputation
Angry spiteful youth with a ball of
Emptiness crying for release
Trigger fingers ready for notoriety bad boys
Needing to move on shooting
To kill breaking windshields slashing
Tires shooting the vulnerable rubbing
Blood into his palms sociopaths bleak
Scary robots wound to maim and cripple
Cruthers short of breath dead in the
Electric chair like a black and white wash
Across the badlands

REQUIEM FOR A DREAM DARREN ARONOFSKY 2000

This dream is one of nightmare psychosis and addiction
It is a frightening picture of idiosyncrasy
Madness and alienation
There is a sense of the tenuous that one can resonate with
Like Sara's repetitively flashing past
Memories of a studio audience appearance
Harry copes with syringes digging
Through the depths of his dermis
Requiem deals with four characters each addicted to
This nightmarish dreamscape in their own way
Placing the characters inside hallucinogenic sequences

Injecting themselves with speed and cocaine on schedule
Drug addiction is rampant the destroyer of many lives
The actors are incredible in the end it is a very sad film
Depicting self destruction brutally in
Slow motion and double time
The repetitive unpredictability of this film is frightening
Requiem for a Dream is a Mass for the dead
Upturned eyes steal a glance of its
Secret splendor and fatal beauty
Dark companions languish in putrescence
Searching for oblivion

SUPERFLY GORDON PARKS JR 1972

Funky soundtrack Curtis Mayfield Freddie's Dead,
Superfly, Pusherman, drug-dealing Kingpins
Saga of Youngblood Priest converts coke to cash to start anew
Deglamorizing drug scene exciting action feeling the rush
Watching the action unfold making a
Statement about the endless
Supply of drugs leading to pain suffering and addiction.
Hard boiled crime drama machismo cocaine consciousness
Best of hot funk and rhythm live music contagious
Action drama financed by African American businessmen
Hot drugs mobile wheels guilty joys and orgies unblessed
He knows tricked out cars with supercharged engines and
hot wheels

ACE IN THE HOLE BILLY WILDER 1951 Kirk Douglas

Charlie Tatum is re-assigned to a
Newpaper beat in New Mexico
A reporter arrives from NY City.
He makes fun of his 60 bucks a week salary
There are no Yankees, No big musicals and no 80th floor
To jump from if the going gets tough. Above a road side
Diner there is a 450 year old cave dwelling. Leo Minosa has
Been pinned by a rock fall for 6 hours. Locals make fun of the
Formation saying this is the mountain of the seven vultures
Tatum knows pretty quickly that he has a big scoop

He positions himself perfectly manipulating key individuals
Like the sheriff who slows things down for Charlie.
The atmosphere is like
A carnival until Lorraine stabs Charlie and Leo hopelessly
Pinned by rockfall to the mountain dies.
Much action takes place
At the diner and under expansive
Circus tents that shade the sun
Suddenly the carnival scatters like a flock of birds without
The laughter. Charlie says, "This is my story keep it mine."
This is a place of hell
Worms' companions break down internal substance a dark
Parade languishes in oblivion appalled by human slime

·

ACKNOWLEDGEMENTS

1001 MOVIES
Baudelaire flowers of evil

DEDICATION
To my brothers Bill and Noah